DEATH SHALL BE
DETHRONED

DEATH SHALL BE DETHRONED
Los, A Chapter, the Journal

HÉLÈNE CIXOUS

TRANSLATED BY BEVERLEY BIE BRAHIC

polity

First published in French as *Le Détrônement de la mort. Journal du* Chapitre Los ©
Éditions Galilée, 2014
This English edition © Polity Press, 2016

Polity Press
65 Bridge Street
Cambridge CB2 1UR, UK

Polity Press
350 Main Street
Malden, MA 02148, USA

ISBN-13: 978-1-5095-0064-2
ISBN-13: 978-1-5095-0065-9 (pb)

A catalogue record for this book is available from the British Library.

Library of Congress Cataloging-in-Publication Data

Names: Cixous, Hélène, 1937- | Cixous, Hélène, 1937- Chapitre Los.
Title: Death shall be dethroned : Los, a chapter, the journal / Hélène Cixous.
Other titles: Détrônement de la mort. English
Description: Cambridge, UK ; Malden, MA : Polity Press, 2016. | Includes
bibliographical references.
Identifiers: LCCN 2015029586| ISBN 9781509500642 (hardback : alk. paper) |
ISBN 9781509500659 (pbk. : alk. paper)
Subjects: LCSH: Cixous, Hélène, 1937---Diaries.
Classification: LCC PQ2663.I9 Z4613 2016 | DDC 848/.91409--dc23 LC
record available at http://lccn.loc.gov/2015029586

Typeset in 11.5 on 15 pt Janson Text
by Servis Filmsetting Limited, Stockport, Cheshire
Printed and bound in the UK by CPI Group (UK) Ltd, Croydon, CR0 4YY

For further information on Polity, visit our website:
politybooks.com

Death Shall Be Dethroned   1

Translator's Notes   67

This little book is the *shadow book* of *Los, A Chapter.**
Its witness and its double.

When I had finished writing-transcribing, sowing, *Los, A Chapter*, I was all fired up, I had just conquered myself and been resuscitated, and finally I was going to get some sleep, whereupon this little book, *the booklet* of *Los, A Chapter*, comes rushing in, telegraphically. I *must* write it. The little book takes charge. An iron hand one can't and doesn't want to escape.

I was astonished: it was alreadythere. It was even an alreadythere. And as is the case for any alreadythere you don't notice it until all of a sudden it is there.

It is the scout and the shadow.

It "creates" itself in short bursts, in the space of a few minutes, in the black dawn of Tuesday August 28. I surrender

knowing that it is (1) living; (2) that it won't be published "in my lifetime." This is the source of its strength. "In my lifetime" is perhaps its title, or "Not in my lifetime."

Within the hour I learn that it is already-living, has been since April (2012), *before*, that is, *Los, A Chapter* took shape, then since Pentecost (there's something Pentecostal about it). Here and there: it lives already here

* Notes about some of the subtleties, lost in translation, of the original French text will be found in the Translator's Notes. They will not be signaled in the text.

1

and there in almost all the notebooks and exercise books that constitute my baggage in time. Notes for it can be found in the Peau d'Âne notebook, in the Giacometti notebook, in the Matisse notebook, in the Beethoven-partition notebook (Isaac gave me this one in 1998, I spend time in it in 1998, 2000, then 2012). During the same period, in ten different scenes under ten roofs, the same mendicant angel taps at ten windows. Interiors closed. Such dispersion speaks of the ghost: it trailed me everywhere with the potent and dogged frailty of a prophet: you don't hear it, you don't hear it, you don't hear it, right up to the day you hear it. The day you cannot not hear it.

A VOICE (*it has the enchanting authority of my father*). – Write me.
A VOICE. – You ought to be scared. You are scared.

Logbook: the register of all the forces that one after another tried to *dissuade* me from writing *Los, A Chapter*. And which, in so doing, made the book, calling it every name in the book.
A book that fought to flee, to keep, Los's name, to stand up for it, attack it, defend it by requisitioning different languages (German, English, Spanish, French). How to not betray it?

(1) This book owes its life to death.

(2) This book owes its life to death. Death also lives.

These reflections stared at each other with melancholy astonishment: hence some books get their life (fire, source) from death. The double taste of Lethe's water: one sip to forget life, one sip to gulp down death. The water of oblivion. Double water. Death and its double and vice versa.

We were sleeping with the dead, Carlos. Your death brings us back to life. Wakes the dreams.

The children

During the summer of 2012, whenever I talk about Carlos with the children it is in the garden under the arbutus tree's branches, it is in a tender, dreamy voice, it is very gentle and telepathic, all three of us are in the same spiritual region, effortlessly we step back forty years, leaning lightly into the same vegetable dream, we haven't changed at all, we savor Carlos's warm and boisterous presence, we haven't changed our minds, forty years haven't tarnished the Los moment, although they have bitten into chewed up sanded down the coast of the ocean we were walking along. Over there, where Carlos stood in his bardic trance summoning the Ocean to open its jaws and release the legend of the other side, no longer exists. The Ocean has swallowed Los's path. If I point to where he stood facing his oncoming book – I saw him from behind, and no one filmed us – that platform of boards and sand is now open sea.

There is no trench of time between the year Los and the year 14. Memory-the-upsurge, memory-the-liar cuts and pastes in a single caress. Our three minds turn with a single smile toward Carlos's great guffaw. At times we were as one, Rue Lhomond, a quick joyous Schubert quartet. From Rue Lhomond 1968 the water of memory swells gently to break over the Atlantic garden 2014, comes to bathe our feet, falls back, goes to stretch out on

5

the American shore, returns, bringing Carlos's indelible luminous ghost. The water rises, with the tide's long, quick, measured stride. To say that henceforth Los is the Enigma's given name, I thought. To think that he was the least enigmatic, the most agreeably transparent of all my inhabitants.

An arbor of trees untamed. Under the dais of mimosas, laurels and arbutus, between the columns of the pines we say the words "the children," "mama," "carlos"; in the false appearance of reality there are three of us, in truth we are seven of whom three actors are embodied in the summer of 2014 – my daughter, my son, me – and four radiant, tenacious subjects – Carlos, my son, my daughter, me – in peak form, in 1969. Chance's light shines on us, there was no misunderstanding, we say the words that don't age, safe childhoods are at play, we address our questions to all ages, sometimes it is my paternal son, sometimes my son the reed the straw adrift among the stars, who answers; now the hair darkens now it is dusted with white.

I was, I am. These five are my witnesses. Their youths watch my youth flash by.

In the neighboring scene Eve shuffles her one hundred years inch by inch toward the goal, she repeats the old soldier's distress call to his impotent commander: help me, help me, help me, help me, help me, little mama. Reader, multiply these notes by fifteen thousand: this is the music of my days. In this scene I am thirty-two years old, I bend over the cradle of my *Uralt* nursling, my soul is in a knot, I say: tell me what I can do for you, I will do it. What do you want? – I don't know, says my ancient, my age-old child.

Broken worn out we creep along the hundred-year-old path, me my mother who calls me mama moaning.

The sorcerers

In my study we are looking for a word. We are seated, all three of us hence all seven of us, the present and the archipresent, and I say: "the oak" and bing! the garden is in the study, for only one oak is "the oak." But for the four of us who are more than present less than present, for the four otherwise present, there is no word yet. I look for it. We look for it. All is spectral, we are all specters. Specter, that's not it. The word *halo* appears, haloes, fans its tail, the wheel fills with images and echoes, but that's not it.

– The past is with us like the present, I say.

– You could say that these four other us-es who are here with us are folded in, thicknesses of the same sheet, says my son. But that's not it.

– We look at each other, we talk to ourselves, we are seven really. Seven equally specters equally present.

– You can't call them "revenants" these beings who stay, who don't return, who don't weaken, who remanate.

– We are the ones who come back, to ourselves, my daughter muses, where this takes place.

– The place is very strong, I say. Every time I go past *La Guitoune*, Carlos opens the window onto the silvery-grey surface of the Bassin, I say. And right away for the thousandth first time we go past *La Guitoune*. Everything is living: everything is going to die. It all goes. It all stays.

7

One is *at the same time.*

This time is a quasi-gnomic present. A present bewitched

– *You ought to be scared.* You *are* scared.

– Yes, I have fears. And I cultivate them. I don't run away from them; on the contrary, since May I have undertaken to live with them as if with cats different from my cats; almost invisible they gallop through the house. As soon as I sit down at my desk, they turn up, shivering transparent cats among my purring ones. It's their muteness that scares me: pure threat. They hiss *Don't*, and dissolve. *Don't!* What an awful word. A performative, an owl cry of fear. Don't! They don't end, don't finish their sentence, they don't say: *Don't* do that! Ectoplasms, they blink and flick off: they themselves, the fears, are afraid of me. "Don't! Don't! You aren't seriously thinking of doing that," they don't say, they vaguely slobber. But my sheet of paper remains impermeable.

I have always been tempted, to the point of execution, by the attraction-repulsion, impulse-repulsion, to head straight for the place I flee. Everything forbidden attracts me. The prohibition is the attraction. The secret is what you are about to tell. "You shall not tell anyone" is an encrypted order. As soon as a thought contains *Not*, it leaps to obey the urgent need to disobey. The Knot tightens.

I first opened the book of the silence of Los around 1981, or maybe 1978–1979 if my memory errs. This is all the more remarkable as Los is a fairly rambunctious sort of being: he emerges like a sea god sputtering from the waves, whipping them with his tail, escorted by a flotilla of dolphins, painters, poets, actors, ambassadors, squiggling shoals among whom he plays the role of a transsexual Cleopatra. And everywhere he goes, as Shakespeare remarks, he makes a gap in nature.

I don't know how I kept such a rambunctious secret intact.

Perfection of that sort demands explanation.

– You didn't keep the secret: Carlos kept it.

– Everything leads one to think that Carlos thought you thought what he thought.

– In truth the secret was kept. The secret decision was taken without anyone ever being told. No one knows when this occurred. No trace. And the secret was as effaced as the secreation.

– Not a word?

– Between me and Carlos, never the word *word*. Hence no non-word. Whereas during the whole time with Isaac words were on our minds constantly, word & company, words of life and of death, words to say in order to not say, so as to say only the words that say differently what they don't say. While in the gossamer space stretched between me and Los I see no word that might have been the last word, no word that could have been *the* word, but I might be mistaken. I'm not mistaken: a mist of error leads me astray: there are some words in the wheatfield C., but the subject H., peradventure or chance, skirts the wheatfield C. without ever crossing it.

I never came up against the idea of breaking the Los silence, the secret law of the Los secret, never entertained the thought of killing the secret, of submitting it to the crowd of questions I will not tolerate being asked, not once in forty years, at least this is what I believe I recall, the questions came along and left again, unanswered. If they came to ask: is there a letter for me? I answered without fibbing: no, none.

A note that pops up again on January 27, 2013, while and because Eve is getting her fill of sleep in the little boat with bars that protects and keeps her from a sudden fall into death, and ferries her between the two worlds, Moses basket of the extremity, and in my head she is already turning into the hunter Gracchus, have you read that, Carlos, I say. No? So I tell him the fable of the posthumous Ulysses who once resembled my father and whose boat my mother now occupies. The Egyptians too take you away in a boat.

I note around, at the bounds of, death. A sacred zone, a mocking zone where neitherlife nordeath confusedly reign, the tiny, potent realm of the Undecided: at one yet-to-be-determined moment a separation will have occurred. You don't separate, you have been separated.

The separation doesn't happen. In place of an impossible separation the sepreparation comes in. The sepreparation is the zone of mists where the suspension of *the willing suspension of disbelief* occurs imperceptibly.

Los and I cite. We like to cite, we invite sentences, characters, myths, to break bread with us. Our guests are the friends we have in common or those only one of us knows and whom we like to introduce to the other.

A smiling story, without any violence, without gloomy underbrush, with big windswept skies, forever already finished. Unfinished

What has brought us together: literature
What separated us: literature
What separates us keeps us
One of us can't stop being perpendicular to Mexico, the other can't stop separating-keeping Ireland, getting as far away as close as possible to France, slipping the English ring on his or her finger
Together for ever in the same separation

We love each other in a language. We love each other in a language in which love plays hopscotch with other languages, leapfrogs, makes-believe, plays the child; that's how it is, love hides and seeks. In what language was the Antony Cleopatra love story acted? His, hers, theirs?

We love each other in English, in a language not mine, not his, that was, wasn't, ours, in which we disembark, arrive, excited, this happened in another life as in a dream, or rather by dreaming, without fail.

The only man known with love without the threat of death. This absence of death, of threat, of terror, everywhere, is impossible.

It can exist only after death; however, in those days no characters were so alive, so swept off their feet by the winds, so flighty, so wantful, so light as her and Los, so amnestied so graced. A thought tells me those two were therefore perhaps survivors unawares, passersby singing in a life beyond. Sparkling with present, flashes of light, fires. Characters detached from the laws of time. *Los.* Spending without counting. Living in the now to infinity. There was to be no bereavement. This can be explained in many different ways. In my view the thing remains very far from the cause. Los.

However, at the same place, not the same place, in the same chapter not the same chapter, into the same play, comes Isaac, pushed onstage by the threatening ghost of *longevity*

Racked, turned on the wheel, drawn between the need

to endure and the dread of enduring, rearing up neighing against the absolute rigidity imposed by the principle of non-contradiction, he is champing at the bit. In his self revolts break out.

When this History can be written, after 2035 or right after my death, they will discover a life full of twists of fate composed of lives full of fateful twists torn up and tossed into Lethe.

In three shouts the ship goes down, *All is lost! Lost!*

(My readers, I have just quoted the opening of *The Tempest*. Everything will always begin with the last word: *Lost*.)

So overnight our life is shattered, we find ourselves dripping wet on an island; for Carlos and me the island is Mallorca, everything our life was and was going to be lies on the bottom, and this everything is now but a brief part of our life. What yesterday seemed to be our eternity has been shown out. And our life, which began every morning with the name of Isaac, to the point of being its synonym, overnight is done

Mademoiselle Albertine has left: a change of book.

My Georges

– What was I telling my heart?
– Ah! That we were sleeping the sleep of the dead along with the dead, Carlos and me. That's when:

Wonderful week of May 2012: one after another all my beloved dead return. Did the rumor get around, on the other side, that the doors between us had opened at Los's approach? I heard from Odysseus that at a Nekyia all the dead come rushing to the phone at once. As if there was but one dead person, who comes back to die and resuscitate at each of the Tragedy's representations.

When I hear that Flaubert is dead I feeling a wrenching sorrow. Yet, or because, I was dreading it, in secret I conjured it up – for months, or weeks – in vain. Still it hits me like a bolt from the blue, like the death of my father, like Carlos's death-bolt.

Always the same pick striking the same tumulus, the opening in the side of the tomb of my life.

This week

(1) relived a whole life in two days, total, with Los, I am thirty, we go round the world, on our return he leaves his mustache scissors in the bathroom for his next visit. Carlos is still thirty-nine years old

(2) relived an awful day with T. (*Todt*), who turns out to be a blind, mad ophthalmologist. In the beginning I was crazy about him. I took him for Isaac. (You can read about this in *Beginnings*)

(3) on Thursday toward midnight my father Georges boards the Brief Dream. He is thirty like me. Then he is thirty-nine like Los. I am ecstatic. We make a film about him. He enters, slender, a little flexible, in a white suit, his slim waist girded by a high, red, revolutionary belt, his eyes long, gazing pensively into infinity, and he leans against the railing as I watch, my eyes ruined with happiness. Extreme beauty. As supernatural as ever. He turns toward the camera and launches into some dazzling discourse, speaking fast; under the influence of his eloquence dozens of voices populate the world with the coming triumphs of Humanity. Despite his death at the age of thirty-nine, Georges my father is still at the peak of his form.

At four in the morning, I realize where this solemn young splendor, lost and found again, comes from. *Its name is Georges.* For a month I've been living with Büchner's genius coursing through my blood. Georges Büchner brings Georges Danton back from the dead Among the young dead georges the word gets around.

December 24, 2011: I "reread" my notebooks from the years 2009, 2010, 2011, then the notebooks Isaac gave me in 2000, 2001 and I notice an inflamed thread, the drunken battle with everything that would keep me from writing *The-Book-I-Don't-Write*. Years, thirty maybe, with this ghost that taunts and implores me. I live with the idea that I will never write it, I live despite this idea or maybe thanks to it. The heart's tumor. Idesolation. Threats. Fears. Along comes Isaac's death, and I live with the idea that each year it grows increasingly impossible to write The-Book-I-Don't-Write, each day perhaps, and even more impossible not to write it. An idea that keeps me from living and keeps me from dying and which, were it to keep me from dreaming, would kill me. However, the other me, the me who inhabits this other life, the one that invents itself independently of my cares and worries beyond the horn and ivory gates, sails on across my shipwrecks, at least until today (December 24, 2012).

I take note: in the other life, in which the other me free of me goes about its business, death, which infects my real life, doesn't exist. This marvelous *dethroning of death*, this death of death, shows me the unreality of this sojourn of mine here where there is no time. On the immortality side, when I am there, death doesn't take life away from the dead. There is a price to pay for this happiness that knows none of the cruel diurnal laws, and is not subject to forgetting, nor to any of the prohibitions that police our existences: the terrible violence of grace. One never has it. One hopes in vain. Suddenly it is granted, and equally suddenly withdrawn. It strikes, grants and takes back. In this country one falls, from this country one is expelled, in a state of *involuntariness*.

My way of "thinking" about The-Book-I-Don't-Write is unbalanced, compulsive, continual, regretful; I moan and groan, it lies flat, it describes circles, by the hundreds, around my beloved's cadaver. I am seeking *the form*. It's like God's Dithering with his ball of mud, the soul and all time are suspended in its god-thorax, all that's missing in order for the creature to take its first breath is *the form* in which to publish it.

In the end the word *form* became my name for god: it had a name and it didn't exist. But, having a name, one day it might.

Inklings. I had inklings.

I thought: I'll never find it. And it's true. You don't find. It may turn up, or the contrary. I see myself posthumous and orphaned: I died before the coming of the messiah. I bend over my tomb in Montparnasse Cemetery with the Messiah at my side and it's too late.

I look for a way out in 2010. Then in 2011. Is it behind me? I dig in my heels: chisel myself a present in the past? No. Present means looking toward the future.

Isaac, when you would say to me, "We are going to find a present," this was – I didn't think of this at the time – a way of making us look toward the future. That was in 1967, as in 2004. In 2001, 1972.

Necessity: find a re-present. Otherwise, lose a life every minute.

Little silhouette of thought in the distance: Gracq's inaudible voice telling-writing me one day that now he doesn't write any more. He was past living.

In Poland, in prison, Döblin escapes from the terrible subhuman labyrinth by the superhuman strength of his imagination: a greatness comes along and saves him, lavishes treasures of active memory on him. "I am warming myself in the sun of everything I see." Welcome, enchantments! The ladders, bars, scaffolds of a house transport him.

Everything comes to me for the first time in the course of an hour in May 2012. Dawn is black. Philia cat, meta-morphosis of a black dawn, strip of night stretched out, lies black and purring at the neck of my white notebook. Suddenly I see it for the first time. Along with Giacometti's drawings, cities, passers-by, bridges, giacomettized build-ings, their souls' elegance, the stupefying fineness of their spines: the first times.

The fifth hour belongs to Philia. A cat-hour. She stretches herself out on my desk, a rival for the paper beings, she unfolds, invades, conceals the ghost pages of *Sodom and Gomorrah* where *sans que, c'en, centaure* are at work, hides, to our left, Walter Benjamin's micrographics, injected at her touch with the power of turning her into a giant; to my right Döblin's violent emotions in Poland, she travels, rolls over on her side so as to steal across the border of the notebook here-open, Philia daughter of Isaac, conqueror of continents, Tyger's descendant.

On two square meters, palimpsestly, broadly over a

hundred sedimented years, myself a sediment of these two centuries which still shift their cities their streets their events in my body

In me, much bigger than me, The Ghost of *The-Book-I-Don't-Write* is riled up: – How much longer are you going to procrastinate?

It never rests.

Under the 2012 notebook of my hesitations, the hyperdense and micrographic layer of the manifesto *Merchandise of Peace* of the year 1923. This powerful yesterday, today almost a hundred years old, reads the text of a M. von *Unruh*! For a second I think it's a joke, that M. Unruh, M. Unrestful, should be a theoretician of peace, echoing Kant's text setting up the sawhorses of perpetual peace. But it is the gentleman's real name.

Years and notebooks I have mislaid. In the end distraction will have taken all my time. Ten years left maybe five. Death will be: the haggard mute figure of my distraction. I see it already.

In literature there is a library Limbo where the books that haven't been written, row upon row of them, are shelved. One meant to write them. Mostly invisible these books are mourned like lost gods by inconsolable readers. The book Joyce didn't write. The book Stendhal meant to write. Dostoyevsky's last. I miss them. I am waiting for you. You were going to exist. Would Kafka ever have written his holy of holies book? And Shakespeare, pregnant with a lord whose sun pants among his planets

The mourning for The Book-I-Won't-Have-Written forms a cyst, glooms. Fondly I recall all the navigators who didn't discover America and who died widowed, all the astrophysicists who, right to the very last minute, awaited their particle.

Don Quixote's fate: one sleepwalks through one's life right to the day one wakes up dead.

I was asleep. A voice jolts me from my dreams. I get up, it is May 16, there is a telegram, addressed to my name, at my address 4 Rue Lhomond Paris-V, this takes place Allée Samuel Beckett, the cats do indeed date from May 2012, but the angel,

the angel has a telegram for a head. This is strange. The age of telegrams ended a long time ago – and yet, it's a fact. The angel is strangely present.

Brief, precise, burning, incredible or credible with a large dose of incredulity

Via Téléfrance – Télégramme

LT Hélène Cixous 4 Rue Lhomond Paris 5 Francia

I *have been sleeping* – and now – now – *I am dead.*

and what flabbergasts me is that it was – or is – signed *in full first name last name* as if there could be any other Carlos but Los. But right away what also knocks me for a loop is the opposite: the unique, sovereign force of the signature. He always signs his messages, letters, telegrams with a calligraphic signature, large, firm, testimonial, open, exuberant, in full, which each time says yes yes it is really and truly me, the receiver, the sender; I respond with my whole body, my whole history, my whole art. Here I affix the seal of my fate. Carlos. The joyful openness of his signature, it's his signature. No doubt about it, he's the one the teacher calls on, Carlos! It really is him, he knows it, there is no other Carlos in the class, any other carloses who might grow here and there in the shade and in the corners are not called upon, the called and so the caller is him. He raised – when? from the age of consent – his so very common name to the height of a king's brow. All the carloses fall in line behind him. Carlos, the original.

I would love to think it's a joke but unfortunately I don't doubt for a moment that this incredible news is true.

In reality only the events for which you are totally unprepared occur: love, death, the revelation of the form of the Book of which I had despaired.

May 28, 2012, a warm Pentecost Monday, I note: this week *I received the Letter*. The Book arrives at the door like the New Angel. It introduces itself. One recognizes it in fear and trembling because one doesn't dare believe, one is embarrassed, one tells oneself it is too beautiful, one is too afraid to be wrong, to be disappointed. Never having seen a New Angel, and yet there's something in the heart that hurries to greet it, that greets it. One would prostrate oneself at its feet, ritually.

Enigmas *forever* wihout response: when I discovered a few years ago, on the Internet, by accident, I no longer know when or how, I wasn't paying attention, wasn't present, that Carlos's archives were at Princeton. A huge repository. One sees *off in the distance*, without commentary, a person whom one has *known*, organizing, a long time ahead of time, colossal obsequies. Known. Already chuckling with fear on his lifebed, running naked before death. Ceremonial. Pyramid. One hundred and twenty-four rooms. The architect of his own tombs. Self-portrait as a royal deathbed scene. Waiting for himself. Setting himself in order. And, *not included* in the legacy to everyone, separately archived, like a P.S. inside, outside, internally excluded, a clause striking in its precision: *all* the rooms are accessible to the public *except* the room with the correspondence.

All the doors are open, *save* the door that is barred. The barring of this door condemns all the others to a common non-condemnation. There is a door devoted to difference. Destined to the contretemps.

The one hundred and thirty-fifth door.

Hardly have these words sprung up under my pen than they acquire a phosphorescent glow. They stand out. Burst into flame like a *Mane Thecel Phares* on the wall to the right of my desk. They leap, in a single bound, to the head of this book. The word Phosphorescence is added, it perturbs me.

– Is it the title?

– It is the number of the secret. Los's secret number to the secret.

– The Secret always has a number. The Secret means to rustle silently. The Secret leaves clues. The Secret likes to give proof of its dissimulation. Most secrets are double agents. Designated by numbers.

They live their seclusion like monks in a time of indefinite relegation, letters returned to post offices not yet in operation. See you later. Some day. See you one of these days, Isaac would say. The idioms' phosphorescence: one of, which, which? Which one, which one of the ones?

Bluebeard's closet. The fruit on the tree of Good and Evil.

You shall not open.

You shall only open too late.

Too late: open, now

La Caja 135

In front of the fauve letter box the guards have been named by Kafka to keep the wild beasts in their cages.

One of my lives cut off from my life lives on in captivity, a fauve phantom boxed up, for years and years.

I heard about this some years ago. In the press. You have a ghost deposited in a Library. A life lifted, that I thought lost or abandoned, locked in a box. Like a relative, a daughter, or me, a stranger, of my ink.

– Where?

– One Washington Road, Princeton, New Jersey 08544 USA

An incalculable mixture of shelter and enclosure: marvelously strange sensation: a me embalmed far from me, if it's "me," raised from the dead, snatched from life and death. Retained. Held naked. But no visitors. It seems we are well conserved, we the ghosts of Box 135, *in special vault facilities.*

So I learn that he *kept* my letters. About the letters I know nothing. The letters that survive us. That take our place, our side, our bed, our throne, which are less us more us than we ourselves. Falsify us, mow us down, perhaps, save us, the lost truth?

How careful Los is, how prudent, in anticipation of what?
How well he protects the beings asleep in the box, as he protects them from us, as he protects us from them. How well he protects the threat, the peace, the violent memory, the feeble force, the excess, the phosphorescence. How well he protects himself.

Carlos Minos. Or Hades: the master of death's doors.

– And you, what have you done with Los's letters? Filed them away?
– I kept the scissors.
The letters – I've left them grazing in time's pastures.
They must be around here somewhere.

We will not open. We will nopen. Too late. One afternoon. A dead day of the year. A day of extinguished star. One will nopen *without ceremony*, the curator declares in a "brief message." Ceremony of the without-ceremony.

El curador de manuscritos

In the forty-fourth month of May after our Mays, hundreds of newspapers mention the tomb box, the press release by Don Tiresias, the curator of the Department of Rare Books and Special Collections, goes global, the fantastic news spreads, a supernatural internaut: it is question of a box, the *Caja 135*, an invention, a gold flake out of Edgar Poe, in which Los's mischievous spirit, an autoprophetic giant, sleeps for a limited eternity. Address: Princeton Archives. A XIXth-century gothic building, Cemetery Bank Credit Memorial Cathedral. It strikes me all of a sudden that the *Caja* is a tale, a fable, a small myth, one of Carlos's ultimyths. Los's gift: everything he looked at always turned in a trice to literary gold. The world is his scenario. It fits in a numbered box whose cipher I don't have.

The forgetbook

Meanwhile, in Paris, not in my writing house, I find some carelessly and firmly kept traces. Coming across them I am filled with admiration for their paradoxical guardianship: at once discreet, absent-minded, trusty and involuntary, this activity has been ongoing and non-existent. Someone in me, therefore, is keeping track, a secret agent as tenuous as his modest and tenacious flock. Just as there is not *a single* universe but as many universes as there are individuals, as Carlos liked to remind us, citing Borges or some or other Proust, similarly, deep inside me, there exists a vast refugee or rebel camp, with whose throngs I mingle passiactively, where acts of resistance are prepared by emulsion. When I join the team that I am, of whom many, though me, are to me cordially unknown, I make my proposals for the operation: great swaths of revolutionary texts and one entire cardboard box, whose dusty, cobweb-veiled state stinks of the crypt's vestibule.

Keptastray: one of Carlos's books shelved within reach. Moldering alongside me on the principle of the purloined letter. When I finally recognize it, forty years of unlikely secret life leap off the shelf where – a slender stow-away my blindness has kept hidden from me – it has subsisted among my so-familiar volumes of Shakespeare and Hugo with the special status of a long-abandoned child, a foreigner to whom systemic carelessness has granted a never-once-verified residence permit. Its fate is as astonishing as that of Figaro: a character of exceptional power, who is everybody and nobody and who has spent an entire lifetime without anyone, himself least of all, wondering where he comes from and what he's doing there.

Unnoticed, unlooked at, unseen, untouched, unmoved, un-, it grew invisible. The way I always know, without knowing, that there is a trace there, a presence omitted, a fossil. Stifled breathing. Preservation in a sort of forgetting-upholstered memory where vestiges abandoned to their fate exist in a vacuum: under arrest. Still alive under the immobile shadows of time.

And yet I-don't-know-who, with the aid of an ancient paralyzed memory, recalls the recluse. Imagine a tiger cloistered for thirty-odd years in a never-visited cage. Each time I have tipped a volume of Shakespeare off the shelf, my right hand must have felt without feeling a mute breath at its fingertips. Through a hypnotized lack of attention my eyes effaced the sight of the foreigner slipped in among people for whom I feel the utmost affection. Right up to the day when the absentee, the bewitched, is suddenly, by magic decree, released. The forgetting is forgotten. The mute bursts out laughing.

This subconscious twilight zone, this pompeii where for an indefinite period of time an under-life dozes: to its streets and hotels come visitors attracted by captive species, sleeping beauties, a populace that waits upon an incalculable decision of fate. A crowd of virtual heroes, the objects of literature's lightning bolts. Characters or objects animated by the probability of life. Their present is forever to come. They wait to be or not to be. Ready. All ready.

I have no idea of the year in which the eruption of ash covered 4 Rue Lhomond and its vicinity with a silky suspension and left everything to chance. One would have to do some research in Los's and my archives.

I have no idea how many of Los's books hide in plain sight, mingle with the crowds on my shelves

My house is haunted, one might say, and that's all one might say. It is one of those tumuli where no people in the world has not felt the urge to build an underground temple. I live accompanied. We are grazed. Now and then, with a start, one of my cats springs up, chomps, sees the soul my own eyes are too weak to see.

Los's books don't move. Don't breathe. They have taken root.

Emphasize *Laughter's* role in my lives. So often forgotten, overlooked, whereas it very often, maybe always, decides the fate of my passions: here I can link two apparently unlinked remarks: how is Carlos different from the other heroes of my book of hearts, just as Passover evening differs from every other evening?

(1) Because he is: "the only man with whom I have lived," that is, *inhabited*, shared a place, an address, dwelt in humanity's primitive cavern, naturally; I mean, the only one with whom I have savored the dishes of before the Fall, the only one with whom I have not trembled, have not known fear; there was no guilt lying around the house, I never heard police on the other side of the door busily nailing down the planks of the courthouse floor and, since there was no ghost, the mask called Fault never crashed through that door, catching us in the act, and thus no wan guest by the name of Innocence was to be found in the apartment either.

He is the only man among men who didn't frighten me with his fear. With his death.

(2) Because he lived his life without a death sentence, he laughed it off.

It's not that Isaac – Isaac who was born of his mother's mocking laugh – didn't laugh, it's that he kept laughter under wraps. On a leash.

Undated: I was ardently in love with T. until one day on a dusty road out of Delphi it hit me that in this brazier there was not even a trickle of laughter. The discovery engendered fear, then revolt or vice versa, then the appalled discovery that the hidden twin of no-laughter was no-dreams. The world had the look of a bone house.

I didn't note the date, but I still see where the lightning struck, the dry white arena without a single echo. We weren't laughing. In the bloodless lips a crack slid its blade of a tongue between us.

My epithet father: deadpan, a *pince-sans-rire*. For his wife "pince-sans-rire" was the height of French chic, the shibboleth, the pince-monseigneur, the housebreaker's crowbar. In German "pince-sans-rire" is pince-sans-rire. My mother is in stitches. "*Dann muss ich lachen,*" says Omi, my German grandmother. "What a laugh," she used to say, whereupon she dealt the indignant adversary *ein-Klatsch*-in-the-face.

These days my mother and I don't laugh much.

– *Passé*, says my mother. – What is passé? I ask.

Passé is an absolute, a long gone. The whole of time and the world is sucked into the unfathomable eras of this word.

– What is past, what has passed? I murmured. The medicine? Or is it she who is gone, sees saw admits to herself she declines, going going gone?

– *Passé!* my mother sighs. – How to write this? Passé? Passer? Passez! Passée? Assez? Passé?

No answer. The response is passé. Response: Past. "*Passé*," the oracle says. Extraordinary. The oracle speaks, in French. In vain I try to translate this word, these syllables, into another language.

One lives, one dies, one loves, one loves or one doesn't love, one is afraid, one wants or one doesn't want, one exists in a single language.

It is a sentence. Isn't it? – The definition of a sentence is that it is a semantically complete statement, my daughter says. – *Passé*: is this a semantically complete statement, is it a statement, is it one, is it?

– *Passé!* my mother the oracle ejaculates.

And no pronoun no subject no address, is there nobody there?

– *Passez.*

I pass, my mother says.

Yet another oracle.

Carlos does not pass.

Carlos, an Albertine, there's the mystery, the incredible thing, these beings are perpetual, people who feign the end. You open a book and there he is, down in the bottom corner of a paragraph, utterly himself, there she is, back again.

Right here, here where I conjure up the Mallorca beach seeing us stretched out like the future's revenants, painted against the beach's sizzle of gold, posed, posing for a distant book that one of us will or will not write, much, much later, while, on the canvas of the moment, we lie here, heat-stunned, submissive to the law of the sky-blue sea that halts passerbys in their steps and pins them to a crystal eternity,

Carlos is there still. Here.

I haven't lost the mustache scissors

Give this some thought. The eminently losable-never-lost object. At constant risk of being lost. Everything I've ever lost: my Isaac nightgown, kidnapped by the laundry service of Manhattan's Gramercy Hotel, I still hear its lament, pleading for help, dragged by the hair like Madame Santeuil's black velour coat, what a nightmare, it weeps in me like a persephone and I cannot retrieve it. It lives for ever in a closet with five hundred other hapless creatures, if it still lives. Meanwhile Carlos's scissors sleep snug in their traveling case.

Lost: in the dark of a hotel room in Trivandrum, my A. jacket, black in the black, my other skin, my armor, my cloak of invulnerability.

Length: 11 cm, long-legged. Converted: from mustache to paper and nails. Strong and gentle. Nogent chrome. With age the chrome has altered, tarnished. But the subject remains as apt as ever. If they could speak? – Japan, India, Canada, Polar Sweden, Senegal, there is no country where I have not cut. I have slept in the same bed with Isaac's pens and A.'s small-squared notebooks.

Fears

In September 2012 I suffer from paradoxical fevers: I struggle to breathe, two fears weigh on my lungs: fear of being read, fear of not being read, fear of suffocating, I feel hollowed out, cavernous. As if in my vital space hostile presences, silhouettes of persecution, crouched. A disquieting inner twilight surrounds my heart. My heart feels foreign, it is a terrified, terrifying someone, who leans out over the railing and doesn't see the stair-well's bottom. The word *fear* tolls like a distant alarm, muffled, abyssal, an eerie rattle, disconnected from its emitter. A growl in the air. With these twin fears at my side, I slide *Los, A Chapter* toward the courts of reading, trembling resolutely, it might be a lamb introduced into the cage where the Lion shudders, guessing it is about to be pushed in to the cage with the Python, it seems girded with the hope of an acquittal, with the powerful and frail hope that we are ready to applaud if it has been a good prophet or to mock and turn our backs if it turns out to have been betrayed.

First, I lay tigerlamb on my free daughter's knee: if she who knows recognizes me, or doesn't, if she who knows how to read pushes the creature away, what then? Then: *Los*. Leaves. What this costs him. Cut.

The panting of Abraham, Isaac's uninterpretable

silence. It is summer, the cicadas are booming. The garden still virgin, without blood.

The verdict, under the tea tree: acquitted. A few wild laurels. *Los* the lamb swiftly nibbles a tuft of grass. The ground is sound, and safe.

Secondly, I send the animal-who-senses-everything to my son, who knows everything. He doesn't read it.

I am afraid of the name, I tell my daughter. What there is in a name. *Los*. A minefield. Arms. Vermin. Occult powers. The dust of fate. The force of the law. A pot of luck.

I flounder in the fens of *Fear, A Chapter*: causes and consequences of *giving* the name. Not giving it. One can't not. If you don't name it, you kill it. The name kills, all the words around it are contaminated.

Problem: everything is in the name, Samson's strength is in his hair, Carlos's in his mustache.

Knife, razor, scissors, lock of hair, fleece

Thirdly, the editor. On page 11, he telephones, "I am on page 11," he cries, all fired up. I check: Carlos is already present on page 11, spelled out, and he is sleeping. The editor says:

*V*ertiginous

*V*irtuosic

Horo*w*itz

I am *v*oiceless

I follow the *V. Le V*? So – ? Saved. And the V goes off. The editor shifts to P:

It's *P*icasso. It's exce*ppp*tional. *P*erfection. Unparalleled . . . words fail me.

Me: –

It is that flamboyant Sunday September 9th, remember? The sky a banner of royal blue, garden wagging
its belly, hundreds of little children skipping down the
paths before all death? The little children: too bad! Bliss:
all that's missing is the crown. No such thing as fear.
There's something about the garden that keeps them in
flight

At the end of this chapter, the obvious: the reader
doesn't know he knows, can't know he knows, that a
Carlos will have existed. Los. Locked out. Keyless.

Just so they don't find the Purloined Letter, is that
what you wanted? Nnn – yes.

Fear for the key: the key to box 135. There is only one.
You are always afraid of losing the key.

On November 9, 2012, a message from fear, a dawn
without light: – Be not afraid of fear. Follow me. I will
lead you into literature's dark depths. Says fear.

I wrote? What did I say? What have I said? Who?
Forget it! I can't answer for her, nor her for me. Gagged,
both of us. We will have been made to shut up, to hear
each other

The day the word *caja* entered my life. The houses that enter our bodies, our brains. What an amazing story: I didn't know I lived in *Caja 135*. The *caja* stripped bare.

Rumor: the conservator declares that some one hundred letters have been kept apart, collected in *Caja 135*. In good condition. Who, dreamless, dozes there? I sleep among the dead. Dead but alive.

September 30, 2012, a thought: he didn't kill me. He shelved me. Decided for me. Played me. Before the *Caja 135* day, I had no idea what had happened: had he decided that that life never existed? What, in the end, would this chapter's fate have been? I might have died without hearing the verdict.

Grace may be granted after the end. In fact it's what usually happens. This is perhaps the contretemps' terrifying charm. It awaits our death to grant us a life that flowers in our absence, at our expense.

A fable. Said to be one of Borges's, unpublished: at the age of sixty-six, from one day to the next, following a premonitory dream, the great writer composes his will. In this notarized letter he asks that the box containing his secrets be kept from all eyes until the first day of the thirty-third spring following the document. Another letter asks that the box be opened exactly two years to the day after his burial. For his burial he gives no date. He has nothing further to say on this topic. The box, small in size, constitutes the one-hundred-and-thirty-fifth part of the great writer's total archives. Naturally all sorts of researchers engage in all sorts of speculations and number games.

We have lived in the last century of the secret. Life in Secret. Hotel Secret. Buried, laid out transparent beneath the sheets of paper.

Such a shelter or tomb will not henceforth be possible. In our story, everything is silenced. Henceforth, all is known, nothing can live in the land of dreams.

I too separated, I am separate from myself, I have gone away, I've remembered myself, I left myself 4 Rue Lhomond, with Los. The keys are in Box 135, 4 Rue Lhomond, in Princeton.

I am missing the day I heard the news on the Internet: the apartment can be visited *in 2021*. In another version the keys can be borrowed two years after the inhabitant's death. *Dos años.*

I recall my stupefaction. We are cards played by a difference engine. I told you about Babbage's difference engine. 2021, the cipher of the enigma. In 2021 you will be ninety-three years old, you will have become a prophetic divinity. Carlos, the hero who opposes the tyranny of Urizen, inventor of the imagination, you will sing *The Song of Los*, blood will turn into perfume and evil into a midsummer night's dream. All the love stories will turn into poems. No one will be the least upset.

One page, somewhere. It wanders for weeks as if no one in me wanted it. Finally we took it in, *here*:

– Talk to me about this silence.

– It was a dual-silence silence. We were two. I imagine they fled one another, resembled each other, feared and appeared magnificently unaware that they'd agreed to remain silent until death, at their own hands, the absolution.

– In the house of years there was a forgotten room, covered in dust, a coat of dust. Somewhere inside me there was a silent but precise but vague consciousness that inside that room lay remains, vestiges never sought, and destined to rot. I have always had a lost city in my life. The ashes erupted in 73 or perhaps 79, that date too has been incinerated, and everything was covered up again, conserved, in ruins. "Like seeds that are dead, but which an idea resuscitates": every time this thought grazed me – but this was so brief – I had the sweet or fearful feeling that Los and I would resuscitate, or die for ever. I cannot even say that I felt this thought (the damp warmth), so eager was I to stamp it out.

She was carved from the mist of despair

– But why, why?

– Two absolutely identical silences. Two mirrors adrift in time's void.

– No last word?

– Two last words, if any are left, under the mantle of paper.

Interrogation:

– Why didn't you ever make a gesture? Say a word?

– Never dared say, speak, evoke C. in front of you, T., in front of you, Isaac, in front of you, A.

– Why didn't you ever?

– And you, why not?

– I don't know.

– Me, Jealousy: I can't speak enough of my role in your lives. I dogged your footsteps, I invited myself on a whim into your happiest hours, I spoiled your lovers' repasts, I spat in your soup, I blew my icy blasts onto your conjoined bodies, in turn I poisoned you, I drip-fed aloe into your hearts, I rolled out the carpet of shadows in the middle of your living quarters. Remember. Remember.

– I remember, alas, I remember: you are nothing but a memory, poor old goddess henceforth no good to anyone. No one left to nip and devour: all is peace. The Disquiet has left them. The me it persecuted is no longer frightened, is no longer on the bitter qui vive in my life.

How I feared you, hated Goddess, how I revolted in vain.

In 73, I live in the reign of Terror. In 74, in 94, in 2000, I am to be decapitated.

By Isaac? By Isaac also, by the beloved.

She shadows us, the denied Goddess.

How I dreaded you, Goddess of the demented, and adored. The threat of you has never left me.

They dared, your faithful, to reproach (suspect, accuse) me for committing the sin they committed, your othellos, they committed the reproach, they convoked the tribunal, my fierce, your haunted ones.

The scene

Seduced. The day Isaac meets Carlos at the painter's, he likes him, he finds him charming, he too is seduced. O wily Eros Shakespeare! We have already experienced this troubling scene. *Carlos*, says Isaac, *is most courteous, a marvelous jester*. O marvelous poet of chance, sower of the seeds of trouble and of discords

At the end of this scene, I hazard a remark:

– Why? Why did you chance it? Why break the seal? Out of a feeling of uneasiness? Out of fear of seeing the silence turn into dissimulation? Or out of . . . ?

I say two words – to acquit myself? To . . . finish? Salute? Hold on to nothing? Recall
    this life has remained intact and perfumed
    thanks to the ashes I remembered every small detail, kept unchanged, for ever mythological, of the garden that time painted on the walls of Rue Lhomond, a paradeisos of strong essences, crowded with laurels, pines, pomegranates, populated with turtle doves and redbreasts,
    the ashes are in a closed room, a little moisture, one warm breath is enough to rekindle them,

    so I say but two words:

"I knew Carlos."

The ashes remain. Isaac's eyelashes, a hint, the thin slit of surprise. Brief spark of displeasure, sudden darkening of the iris. "Knew."

– It was when you were gone, that twelve months' sentence, that yearlong sentence I thought was for ever. It was when. At the knot. At the cruel, poisoned knot of our story. The year without when. Seven years. That year expands – as far as belief can see. The Satan year we were under ground.

– So you couldn't ever just stay by yourself? Black tulip irises gather to themselves seven darknesses of depth.

I didn't say: – Did you ever "stay by yourself," *dear? O my soul's joy after every tempest.*

This scene took place a short time before the death. It might never have happened.

Fleeting, the May 20, 2012 meditation:

In the week that followed the now immortal May 15, 2012, Jealousy was buried. It was an enchanted burial: all my dearly beloved, my children, my friends, all those I have thrice made kings, queens or kingqueens in my life, my cats, all the vibrant creatures adored therefore stung by the poison dart, accompanied a marvelous cortège straight out of *A Midsummer Night's Dream*. Humankind's enemy was laid in a shoebox placed on a chariot veiled with veils, gauzes, percales from Proust's bed-reading room and drawn along the Boulevard Edgar Quinet by members of the Globe Theatre company.

As we sang and danced toward Montparnasse Cemetery, everyone's Hotel de la Paix, and I was holding I was held by my son and daughter with whom, on life-and-death occasions, I form a single being, we all felt a sense of lightness regained. The modest, prudent joy of freshly pardoned prisoners. You are free, healed, you can't believe it's true, quick, you relish it.

An entire life under the sign of Jealousy came to an end on May 16th. Until May 15th you are sealed. Mystery: how on May 16th you can tell yourself that you have loved. How you can feel a sort of love-barred-shown-to-the-door, dismissed, breathe all of a sudden slip in, taking advantage of the absolute interruption of all existence to come forward, as if amnestied by death, as if death pardoned, as if death put an end to the ghosts, banished persecutions. The debt paid off? But that's an illusion. An illusion? Yet the cortège descends the boulevard under the acute blue sky, Jealousy sleeps, its waspish body wrapped in white silk, Madame Iago poisoned my life, she bewitched Isaac, T., J., G., she hurt, bit, betrayed, robbed us

she sleeps, our enraged companion, such a small insect. Some day I could make a list of the murderous scenes she authored, that plague, among which I'll include the big scene in New York, one in Bonn, one in 2000 that exploded on the edge of the Garonne and continued on all the way to the Ocean's sands. I could write a book.

With the title *Isaac Assassinated*. As to who assassinates who, that's a question that would remain open.

Here I would gladly open a dormer window onto the extraordinary story of the Montparnasse Cemetery Hotel. The hotel exists in reality. But it is a supernatural reality. Which is what makes me think twice about mentioning it. Telepathy is a more powerful magician than we would like to think since, without anyone giving anyone else the word, without any consultation or conniving, since they hadn't met each other, all the friends and guiding stars of my life turned up there one after another as in one of Julio Cortázar's fantasies. That we should all have been super-dreaming in the same neighborhood, that we should have gone on spinning our webs under the same dais, I could never have imagined.

Someone, who? Monsieur Probability or Madame Chance, or Master Jabberwocky, some force, must have sent an invitation to each of the voyagers in the Book-I-Don't-Write. Everyone came.

Except for Isaac. Forever dancing to a different tune.

Los could have killed the letters, shredded them, burned them, tossed them whole or in pieces into the river, disguised and transposed them into a short story, thrown them into a box, a drawer, forgotten them in a file forgotten in his room, one of the twenty rooms of his life, or left them c/o Mme Calypso, entrusting her to keep them, while waiting to return on some yet-to-be calculated date, never effacing the traces of their existence, being careful to declare somewhere having committed this act of destruction, of letters hence of life, in a fit of terror or of anger or of madness, and right afterwards regretting it or quite the contrary,

a declaration that he will have inscribed many years later across the top of a page, as if telling the reader a secret, which could be true or false, and which will have that undecidable status of certain of the statements that contribute to literature's troubling charms, thus

he will have had the opportunity to join the freemasonry of poet players of the Game of Letters, postmen, mailmen, thieves, navigators, the exiled devoted amateurs of the contretemps, false true counterfeiters, willingly and voluntarily subjected to the cruel laws of delay, tardiness, the too-lates, all the figures of destiny as strategy of the unexpected, trembling subjects of the laws of chance, drunken bettors on the absolute Throw of the Dice: will I ever receive this letter? Did I ever love you? Did he ever wed her? I shall never know.

When did the *Caja 135* come into being? The idea of the *Caja*? How long did it live?

When was it opened? Closed? Sealed?

When did it leave Carlos's house?

What dreams, what thoughts, what letters, accompanied, determined the creation of the *Caja*?

49

What does the *Caja* bring to mind? Allusion? Box, safe, tomb, locker, vault, crypt, Dr Frankenstein's laboratory, Dr Faustus's office, Edgar Poe's raven's nest, Jules Verne's unfinished posthumous hive of a novel, a fake novel by Borges, Cortázar's manuscript of the Dream Manuscript? A mummy box. A chrysalid case. A barrel of explosives. Dried flowers

Who is writing these letters preserved under the heading of my name? Should my homonym's scribbling bother me? Worry me? Threaten me? Reassure me?

Have you ever received, eight years after his death, a letter from a dead friend or a dead lover or someone you loved who has died, written a decade at least before his death and which comes to you care of your publisher?

The envelope is elegant. The message knocks you for a loop.

Never-More: the posthumous name of the beloved who departed without answering the last question. Nevermore.

An unpublished story by Henry James: the sickly narrative is waiting for the opening of the box that contains the secret letters, and probably the last word, of her beloved poet. She doesn't want, or is unable to die, or finish, before she hears this word. She holds her breath. But one day, tempestuous or exhausted, the narrative dreams that she is present at last at the crypt's opening: the crypt holds nothing. I repeat: the crypt is empty. The narration utters its last cry.

Some people wonder if the box could be opened *before* the death of the legator. Some wonder what the box's secret force is. Let's imagine that the great writer during his lifetime sees the final date for the box's safekeeping approach. What will he choose to do? Will he hold himself, living, for dead? For how long? What meaning, value, duration, function, do we accord to this two-year lapse of time supposed to separate the closing (or opening) of the tomb from the opening (or closing) of the box? What will, what must happen in those two years, who will *Los* have been? What or who will have: ceased, begun, stopped, changed, finished dying, suffering, trembling? In two years.

What is a burial of predetermined indeterminate length?

The person departed, the letters resuscitated, the letters sent off to arrive after death. The right of life in death. Death? So full of life, of lives.

A cardboard box, *cast up* on my topmost shelves, an ark of letters beached on a barrow of earth: Hantaï, Genet, Gracq, Leclerc, Carlos. Among the dead, he alone was alive. Had this ever occurred to me?

Sitting beside the ark with the living letters of the dead, the great tiger of the Peking Opera, its sunburst head bent toward its right shoulder, its sardonic smile each time Isaac glances over at it saying: What? How long has it been there, watching us? And then saying again: Was it there the last time? I still hear his amazement at not having seen, at seeing for the first time the effigy that he sees each time for the first time. This tiger has a secret: it exists only in the instant, in the autumn of the day, when we are making love,
   as if the idea brought it back to life

A *Lettre de Privilège*: two years day for day after death, one will have the right to be, to have been. On the other hand, one's right to mystery will cease.
   – We'll meet when both of us are dead.
   – When will we be dead, Los, when will we meet again?
   – Two years after your death.
   – Two years after, our death.
   Make sure we are dead but not for too long: something Isaac and I have more than once experienced.

The first time I ask Isaac when we will return for the first time, he replies without hesitation, "in fifty years"; we lie side by side, connected by the body of our cat stretching itself out along our legs. Isaac gazes toward the pinnacles of the bookshelves, where the tiger's smile keeps its eye on us.

Another year, when I ask him the same question for the second time, we are sitting on the little divan, the two cats are black at our sides, the two crows white at the window, knowing full well there could be no once-and-for-all answer he says: "in thirty years" or perhaps "when we are ninety." Will we ever be ninety? In how many centuries will we be ninety? In how many dreams?

We were in exile and we were laughing.

The idea of adding to Carlos's laugh comes to me at 5 o'clock on the black, cold morning of March 10, 2013, a month in which I have only laughed once (see below), a month whose not-laughing has parched my skin and contracted my muscles, a month I cross like a camel that has been deprived of a chance to drink long and deep before being driven into the Sahara's long furnace. "We're going to die." He said this roaring with laughter right from the source when he returned from his disastrous spring trip to Prague, where he – a visitor already in exile – saw himself coming to record the start of another exile in the Czechoslovakian mirror. Dictatorships were erecting walls as fast as they could, and hope prowled the ramparts like an abandoned dog.

About the Laugh: I had almost reached such a state of dryness that even *the idea* had withered and yellowed and stopped stirring in my head.

This idea, this laugh, was revived in me after a chance reading one night of *The Hessian Courier*. Büchner's laugh was only yesterday, I thought; after all, there are fewer than a hundred years between Büchner, the flame and the voice, and Eve my mother. A hundred years, a mere two chapters in the history of the republican continent's joyous respiration. Between Büchner and my mother, the hyphen, the wave of a laugh of survival, the laugh of liberation.

– By chance, you say?

– Or the contrary?

The laugh of liberation, one hears it roar in these frontier cities, these zones of refuge where all those who flee arrest leave traces of their flights.

Each time I go to Strasbourg I go in 1914 to see my mother running through the same streets where Büchner passes, I go in 1835, I go in 1994, I go in 2000, every time with the most violent feelings, I take the same streets with Isaac, one day coming out of the Red Hat Hotel I find myself nose to nose with Vassilikos, we burst out laughing, crossing the street we have just skipped forty years. The same laugh, the laugh of liberation.

We were laughing. I was going to forget to say so. Those years fresh as nymphs dabbling in the infernal rivers, mythological years: no one with a home of their own any longer, no home of my own, each with an image of the stolen country like a photograph tacked to the wall in a hotel room of the heart.

Hotel Greece, Grand Hotel Argentina, Hotel Mexico, Hotel Havana, Hotel Spain and the Baleares. Grand Hotel Madrid Place of Three Cultures. Mexico.

With all our heart we laugh. We find ourselves, each other, droll, all of us out, shown the door, a band of the expelled. The expropriation purifies us. All these shivering, roofless selves peddling ruses and uprisings, word-buskers. No one to be president. No one to be ambassador, each only a poet child and co-seer. These are days of lightness, without fear for tomorrow for there are no tomorrows, there is only one day in the Years of Exile, and the whole world is equally orphaned. Families are constituted and added to around a raft moored to the terrace of a café. We love each other, we aren't hurting anyone, there's an abundance of admiration for everyone, and we congratulate one another on our good luck. This is Illyria. The cast of characters gathered in the enchantment of those years of summer, when I reconstitute it from afar, brings to mind the adorable squadron of angels Proust Giotto envisioned on that midnight he painted them, in under two hours, hovering against the stone sky over the terrace where the scene of Christ's lamentation was being acted. When Carlos brings me a postcard from Padua we are struck by the resemblance between the scene that took place in 1306 and the one at Christmas in 1967. Present in the chapter, Rue des Grands Augustins: Julio Cortázar, Ugné Karvélis, Marie José Paz, Octavio Paz, Vassilis Vassilikos,

Mimi Vassilikos, Italo Calvino, Carlos, Piotre Rawicz, and the painter. And those I've forgotten.

If on earth one weeps, on the stone blue sky a group of five ageless imps describe magical circles. The lamentation on the closed ground of a parapet is supposed to be the painting's subject. In fact it is the acrobatics of the pint-sized angels in the top half of the painting that is this event's high point. I write these lines in one of those lives in the afterlife

Dream wisdom 1

On February 16, 2013, a great surprise: Carlos is back! Carlos himself. Loud (at least compared with my murmur), truculent, curious, joyful. I am glad. I am embarrassed. He turned up, bouncing with life, smack in the middle of the street I was crossing. The problem is he knows nothing, obviously, about my present life. (Nor I about his.) These days I am perhaps with the king. It would be one of our secrets. But, being in the street of dreams, I will be with him. Los! How fresh his name! On my tongue. I must take a moment to clear things up with him. I want to. Yes I want us to make love and use the word *love*. But first I will tell him. We can tell each other. That we can tell each other. That we were able to tell each other is the mark of our lives. He throws his arms around me. He laughs. Laughing is his sign. His punctuation. He comes bearing gifts. His baggage: the English trunks. Pat them, they yelp. It is moving to hear the trunk sound again. From his trunks, he pulls two big paintings I see only the backs of. His: he has signed and dedicated them. I am looking a little older. What if he finds the skin of my upper arms all crinkled and loose? I don't show my concern. He sniffs me. As usual. He puts his arms round me. I have an epiphany: our life dances. Is a dance. Crowds of people high in color, in nature, stream by. These people don't think twice about undressing and walking past us on the sidewalk, men, women, tanned, copper-colored, Irish, Argentinean, some have thick legs, but who cares,

When Carlos comes back, it is truly our very own Carlos, our joyful lover, our innocence, our gourmand. Who wins out over the worried, worrying, morose Carloses who come from Calderón to darken the corners of daily life, with whom I frighten myself, the demi-monde Carloses. Our Carlos purchases armloads of flowers, sketches children with a deft hand, I'd forgotten that he has also bought baskets of fruit and vegetables, he puts one of them in my arms, he is quick, renewed, intact, glittery as a serpent that has sloughed its skin. Curious. I'll tell you, I say. I want us to spend these carefree days together. Oh, this book of May. We pick it up again in the next chapter. The characters are waiting for us. Nothing has changed in the voices, the sentence unwinds its long thread. We were right *here*.

Wisdom of Dreams. It is a kingdom without death, without resentment. Criminality is rare, friendship elastic. As if by chance during these days the dreams discover traces I was unaware of. I suddenly speak a language I didn't know I knew. Taking down an old volume of the Pléiade, look, written in my hand at the top of a yellowing page, a remark by Carlos saying he is happy. On the verso I note that I swing from credulity to incredulity. It comes to me that my Los-Life has all the characteristics of a dream. The idea comes to me in a dream self-evident as truth

Dearly beloved Isaac, between January 10 and March 25, 2013 there is a blank page in our Life-after-life. The whole time I was busy with the *shadow book* of *Los, A Chapter* the Isaac Dreams stayed away.

I am struck by the absolute singularity of this withdrawal: between 2010 and 2013 Isaac visited me eighty-nine times, intermittently, it is true; he might turn up three or four times in a fortnight, and then make me wait but never for longer than three weeks. I reacted to these occasional delays with unremitting anxiety and, the utter uselessness of such prayers notwithstanding, I pleaded with him to return, and not to inflict upon me an absence that was too much like punishment; naturally he never came back on demand but, as in reality, as soon as I was no longer counting upon his return, he would pop up, and then always with the joyful and reassuring energy that makes what I call "Isaac's returns" shine with the luminosity of sunrise, the kind of proof of the existence of God-in-whom-one-doesn't believe, and always with the sort of restorative breeze, the saving breath, that follows and sweeps away a period of suffocation; in no time our life resuscitated, and death ceased. I should emphasize that these harsh but limited eclipses have for me always been painful and incomprehensible. They saddened me; they were like the suffering associated with the daylight eclipses brought about, when we were alive, by the hostile eruptions of Jealousy, goddess of murders and interrogations. Each time I'd have to call for the help of the clear, precise protestations of innocence and the oaths of fidelity that Isaac formulated more than once, consigning them to paper, and sealing them with a solemn word and a smile, so as to relieve the burn that the inexplicable discontinuity caused. And when it was over, when Isaac was found again, it was ravishing, it was as if no wound had scarred our time together, there was no trace, it was as if the pain had never existed, we were brand new, we were walking as usual on the beach, listening together to the eternal song of the rising tide.

Well, during that season when I lived a life full of sunshine, and Carlos was the sun, for seventy-four days there was not a shadow of a visit from Isaac, as in that far-off season whose long quick months were chock-a-block with revolutionary action, when cities were turned inside out and emptied like fallen armoires, months when I didn't see Isaac, I was capable of not seeing him, Isaac, I could, one noon at the corner of Rue d'Ulm and Rue Lhomond, just as I was jumping over a barricade, encounter Isaac coming toward me in person as if from the depths of a mirror and I said, with astonishment: "You, here!" as if this sudden meeting was the most unlikely thing in the world. As if no one but Isaac could be so far from my thoughts, as if no one could be less expected than Isaac in this topsy-turvy world that Carlos was racing through, as if, through an unseen crack in the wall, the being-in-the-world who among us had the least chance of coming back – had never even had ghost status – had suddenly extracted himself from nothingness and slipped bladelike through my gaze before I had even set eyes on him.

"You, here!" I cried. Like that: You! Here!
I say to my daughter. We are sitting at the golden

yellow table of the year 2013 and I still hear the ex-plo-sion of those words on the lips of Rue Lhomond 1968. I was able to say those words? I am still utterly amazed. – Do you hear this *You* go off? I ask my daughter. The shot rings out.

– "You," an antonymic pronoun, says my daughter. You couldn't have said that in English, my daughter says. – I only ever loved Isaac absolutely in French, I say, I told him You! You? I was stunned. – As a result it is not only an interlocutory pronoun, it is also the pronoun of interpellation. – I was calling out to him, I didn't believe it, I didn't believe my eyes. I shouted: You! What a sentence! – "You" is a pronoun-sentence. Behind "you" lurks the ghost that causes us to doubt. It's you, You? I shouted. That is you *there*? I mean: here, on this street corner? I can't get over it. How I wasn't expecting you! Either I was delighted, or I was shaken. Only God turns up like that. God in whom we have stopped believing. – Or perhaps You is an apostrophe. A performative: the moment you utter: "God!" there he is at the door, he is already in the entrance. – And I said: You! And I made Isaac appear and, with the very same word, I summoned him. I didn't say: "What are you doing here, You?" but I might as well have. Your appearance is out of place, and right away everything else is displaced, the street, the time of day, what I believed to be – past. – It's interrogation and exclamation, both, says my daughter, the grammar book. The exclamation is a grammatical marker. It is as if Isaac said to you: You, here! Who knows who hits who. There is an explosion. You! Pow! – What force! The fewer the words the greater the impact. – Nobody in the street, it wasn't his place. – Nobody. In his place.

On his face, vexation.

At these two words, proffered in a voice utterly foreign to the life that had been, one saw to what point it no longer existed. I was no longer expecting the Isaac-life in this world, as usual I had had faith, faith itself, unshaken, docile, obedient, confident, in the law decreed by him, I always believed, always followed it, to the letter and in every way, sort of.

(I'd said: You, here?! At the corner of Rue Lhomond and Rue d'Ulm. For ever afterwards I avoided that damned spot. Where I had doubted.)

On March 25, 2013 when I wake, I find a spyglass on my pillow: see how I watch my nights! This makes me laugh. I get up hugging my pillow to show it to you. We are at the start of our story which is destined to last till the end of our days. Here I am on my knees between your knees, Isaac, with my spyglass, I spy your lovely face, Isaac. I notice that you came to France before me, to wait for me.

It's the Surprise. You have been nominated by the Dream of dreams, and you have agreed to take up the position.

Could I really not have dreamed of you for so long, not have called you, go for so very long without looking at you? Agreed to-not-frighten-myself, not find you in night's and the notebook's corner? Without undergoing the pain and the feelings that dare not say their names? And all the while as if alive?
Surprise: that you be named a prince by the Dream-u-versity
and now I find you again, surprise, in the little square waiting room of the University of Dreams

Surprise: that without a second thought, and without a word, we fall into one another's arms
that we tumble joyfully to the ground

that the gap be closed and absence returned to absence
without a trace of a cut or seam or of the months that
came between our two books, during which I neither
dreamed about or sought to see you, I neither suffered
nor rejoiced in suffering

and that the enchanting months of the Los chapter of
my life, which held a sweetness, and beneficial lightness,
a wholly innocent youthfulness, where one breathed an
air inevitably scented with oleander and orange blossom,
should have dissipated during the night of March 24 to
25, 2013. I felt them slipping away from me with that all-
powerful, humanly irresistible retractability of dreams,
I felt a little mist seep from my heart, last vapor, last
breath, as they settled deeper into the kingdom without
a country where memory returned to oblivion in my bed.

On this Monday March 25, 2013 Isaac came back,
exactly as in reality, once again, in the world that I carry
within.

One doesn't die. One comes and goes between two
absences of memory.

TRANSLATOR'S NOTES

I wish to thank Hélène Cixous for her elucidations and suggestions while the translation was in progress. All errors of omission or commission are entirely my own responsibility.

shadow book (page 1): in English in the original French text here and below.

Los, A Chapter (page 1): see Hélène Cixous, *Abstracts and Brief Chronicles of the Time: I. Los, A Chapter*, trans. Beverley Bie Brahic (Cambridge: Polity, 2016).

under ten roofs (page 2): in French *sous dix toi* in which *toi* ("you," second person singular) echoes *toits* ("roofs").

The water of oblivion (page 3): in French *L'eau d'oubli*, which echoes the sound of *Eau double* ("Double water").

help me (page 6): in French *aide-moi*, in which the first two letters *ai* ("ayee") are italicized.

The Knot tightens (page 8): in French *Le Noeud sert*, in which *Noeud* ("knot") echoes *Ne* ("not") in the previous sentence and *sert* suggests both *serrer* ("tightens") and *servir* ("has its uses").

the hunter Gracchus (page 10): the title of a short story by Franz Kafka in which the protagonist drifts between life and death.

the willing suspension of disbelief **(page 11):** in English in the original.

so flighty, so wantful (page 12): in French, playing with the sounds of the two words: *plus volants, plus voulants*.

All is lost! Lost! **(page 13):** in English in the original.

Beginnings **(page 16):** see Hélène Cixous, *Les Commencements* (Paris: Grasset, 1970; reprinted by Des femmes–Antoinette Fouque, 1999).

Merchandise of Peace **(page 20):** Cixous's reference to the *Merchandise of Peace* manifesto is drawn from "Micrographies" in *Walter Benjamin Archives* (Paris: Klincksieck, 2011, pp. 66–7) (email communication from Hélène Cixous).

von *Unruh* (page 20): Fritz von Unruh, a German writer and Nazi opponent. In German *unruhe* means "unrest," "alarm," "disquiet."

Allée Samuel Beckett (page 21): this is a section of the Avenue René-Coty in Paris's 14th arrondissement.

I *have been* . . . I *am dead* (page 21): in English in the original.

the door that is barred . . . condemns (page 23): in French "a barred door" is *une porte condamnée*, allowing for a wordplay that does not exist in English.

Mane Thecel Phares **(page 23):** the writing on the wall in the biblical Book of Daniel 5:25–6.

in special vault facilities **(page 25):** in English in the original.

curator of . . . Collections (page 26): in English in the original.

the *Caja* is a tale (page 26): "a tale" in English in the original.

pince-sans-rire **(page 32):** to keep a straight face while joking.

pince-monseigneur (page 32): a crowbar, or tool used by housebreakers, from *pince* ("pinch") and *monseigneur* ("milord").

Passé! . . . **Passé? (page 33):** all these words are variations on the verb *passer*, whose meanings are legion, from the obvious "to pass" to *maison de passe*, a brothel. *Passé* is the past participle, and so is *passée* but with a feminine instead of a masculine ending. *Passez!* is an imperative. *Assez*, or "enough," is linked to *passez* through rhyme.

fear of not being read (page 37): in French – here truncated, for lack of a satisfactory translation – *peur de n'être pas lue* ("not be read") chimes with *peur de naître* ("to be born") *pas lue*.

A pot of luck (page 38): or, as French has it, "a bowl of luck." (A French idiom *avoir du bol* means "to be lucky," but in English there is a pot at the rainbow's end.)

I follow the *V*. *Le V*? So – ? Saved (page 38): in French, playing on the sound of *le V* (pronounced *le vay*): *Je suis le V. Lever? Levé. Levée. Sauvée.*

The Song of Los **(page 41):** in English in the original.

"Like seeds . . . resuscitates" (page 43): cf. Marcel

Proust, "Notes sur la literature et la critique," in *Contre Sainte Beuve* (Paris: Gallimard, 1971), p. 303.

Remember. Remember (page 44): in French, *Souviens-toi. Sou-viens-toi.* The breaking of the word into its syllables emphasizes its three components: Under/come/you.

is most courteous, a marvelous jester **(page 45):** in English in the original.

as far as belief can see (page 46): in French *à perte de croyance*, an expression based on the French idiom *à perte de vue* ("out of sight, as far as the eye can see").

dear? O my soul's joy after every tempest **(page 46):** in English in the original (cf. *Othello*, Act II, Scene 1).

Never-More … Nevermore (page 50): the second "Nevermore" is in English in the original and echoes Edgar Allen Poe's "The Raven," a poem which fascinated French poets such as Charles Baudelaire and Stéphane Mallarmé.

Lettre de Privilège **(page 53):** under France's Ancien Régime, editors might receive from the King the exclusive right to publish a book for a certain period of time, protecting them from competition. The *Lettre de Privilège* was thus an ancestor of copyright.

The Hessian Courier **(page 55):** a political treatise written by Georg Büchner in 1834.

use the word *love* (page 59): "*love*" in English in the original.